To renew this book, phone 0845 1202811 or visit
our website at www.libcat.oxfordshire.gov.uk
You will need your library PIN number
(available from your library)

OXFORDSHIRE
COUNTY COUNCIL
SOCIAL & COMMUNITY SERVICES
www.oxfordshire.gov.uk

3302747471

FRANCIS FRITH'S

OXFORDSHIRE VILLAGES
PHOTOGRAPHIC
MEMORIES

THE FRANCIS FRITH COLLECTION

www.francisfrith.com

FRANCIS FRITH'S

OXFORDSHIRE VILLAGES

PHOTOGRAPHIC MEMORIES

LES MAPLE is retired and a freelance writer. He is the Long Distance Path Information Officer for the Long Distance Walkers' Association, a member of the Outdoor Writers Guild, and is currently Secretary of the Thames Valley Group of the LDWA. He was born in Burry Port, South Wales, but he moved to England in 1967 to work with computer systems. Since 1977 he has lived in Windsor with his wife. He is a keen long-distance walker, and is interested in the outdoors generally. He contributes regular articles to 'Strider', the journal of the LDWA. Other books he has written include: '100 Walks in Berkshire and Oxfordshire' (1996); 'Around Windsor' (2001); and 'The Long Distance Walker's Handbook' (co-editor, 7th edition 2002).

FRANCIS FRITH'S
PHOTOGRAPHIC MEMORIES

OXFORDSHIRE
VILLAGES

PHOTOGRAPHIC MEMORIES

LES MAPLE

First published in paperback in the United Kingdom in 2011 by
The Francis Frith Collection®
ISBN 978-1-84589-558-7

British Library Cataloguing in Publication Data

Oxfordshire Villages - Photographic Memories
Les Maple
ISBN 978-1-84589-558-7

The Francis Frith Collection®
Unit 6, Oakley Business Park,
Wylye Road, Dinton,
Wiltshire SP3 5EU
Tel: +44 (0) 1722 716 376
Email: info@francisfrith.co.uk
www.francisfrith.com

Aerial photographs reproduced under licence from Simmons Aerofilms Limited
Historical Ordnance Survey maps reproduced under licence from Homecheck.co.uk

Printed and bound in England

Front Cover: **BROUGHTON**, *The Saye and Sele Arms 1922* 72116t
The colour-tinting in this image is for illustrative purposes only,
and is not intended to be historically accurate

Frontispiece: **BENSON**, *Bensington Weir 1893* 31704

Every attempt has been made to contact copyright holders of illustrative material.
We will be happy to give full acknowledgement in future editions for any items not
credited. Any information should be directed to The Francis Frith Collection.

AS WITH ANY HISTORICAL DATABASE, THE FRANCIS FRITH ARCHIVE IS CONSTANTLY BEING
CORRECTED AND IMPROVED, AND THE PUBLISHERS WOULD WELCOME INFORMATION ON
OMISSIONS OR INACCURACIES

CONTENTS

FRANCIS FRITH: VICTORIAN PIONEER   *7*

OXFORDSHIRE VILLAGES - AN INTRODUCTION   *10*

SOUTH OXFORDSHIRE   *14*

MAPLEDURHAM FROM THE AIR   *16*

ORDNANCE SURVEY MAP OF DORCHESTER   *32*

NORTH OXFORDSHIRE AND THE CHERWELL VALLEY   *52*

THE OXFORDSHIRE COTSWOLDS   *74*

THE VALE OF THE WHITE HORSE   *88*

OXFORDSHIRE COUNTY MAP   *114*

INDEX   *115*

Free Mounted Print Voucher   *119*

FRANCIS FRITH
VICTORIAN PIONEER

FRANCIS FRITH, founder of the world-famous photographic archive, was a complex and multi-talented man. A devout Quaker and a highly successful Victorian businessman, he was philosophical by nature and pioneering in outlook.

By 1855 he had already established a wholesale grocery business in Liverpool, and sold it for the astonishing sum of £200,000, which is the equivalent today of over £15,000,000. Now a very rich man, he was able to indulge his passion for travel. As a child he had pored over travel books written by early explorers, and his fancy and imagination had been stirred by family holidays to the sublime mountain regions of Wales and Scotland. 'What lands of spirit-stirring and enriching scenes and places!' he had written. He was to return to these scenes of grandeur in later years to 'recapture the thousands of vivid and tender memories', but with a different purpose. Now in his thirties, and captivated by the new science of photography, Frith set out on a series of pioneering journeys up the Nile and to the Near East that occupied him from 1856 until 1860.

INTRIGUE AND EXPLORATION

These far-flung journeys were packed with intrigue and adventure. In his life story, written when he was sixty-three, Frith tells of being held captive by bandits, and of fighting 'an awful midnight battle to the very point of surrender with a deadly pack of hungry, wild dogs'. Wearing flowing Arab costume, Frith arrived at Akaba by camel sixty years before Lawrence of Arabia, where he encountered 'desert princes and rival sheikhs, blazing with jewel-hilted swords'.

He was the first photographer to venture beyond the sixth cataract of the Nile. Africa was still the mysterious 'Dark Continent', and Stanley and Livingstone's historic meeting was a decade into the future. The conditions for picture taking confound belief. He laboured for hours in his wicker dark-room in the sweltering heat of the desert, while the volatile chemicals fizzed dangerously in their trays. Back in London he exhibited his photographs and was 'rapturously cheered' by members of the Royal Society. His reputation as a photographer was made overnight.

VENTURE OF A LIFE-TIME

Characteristically, Frith quickly spotted the opportunity to create a new business as a specialist publisher of photographs. He lived in an era of immense and sometimes violent change.

For the poor in the early part of Victoria's reign work was exhausting and the hours long, and people had precious little free time to enjoy themselves. Most had no transport other than a cart or gig at their disposal, and rarely travelled far beyond the boundaries of their own town or village. However, by the 1870s the railways had threaded their way across the country, and Bank Holidays and half-day Saturdays had been made obligatory by Act of Parliament. All of a sudden the working man and his family were able to enjoy days out and see a little more of the world.

With typical business acumen, Francis Frith foresaw that these new tourists would enjoy having souvenirs to commemorate their days out. In 1860 he married Mary Ann Rosling and set out on a new career: his aim was to photograph every city, town and village in Britain. For the next thirty years he travelled the country by train and by pony and trap, producing fine photographs of seaside resorts and beauty spots that were keenly bought by millions of Victorians. These prints were painstakingly pasted into family albums and pored over during the dark nights of winter, rekindling precious memories of summer excursions.

THE RISE OF FRITH & CO

Frith's studio was soon supplying retail shops all over the country. To meet the demand he gathered about him a small team of photographers, and published the work of independent artist-photographers of the calibre of Roger Fenton and Francis Bedford. In order to gain some understanding of the scale of Frith's business one only has to look at the catalogue issued by Frith & Co in 1886: it runs to some 670 pages, listing not only many thousands of views of the British Isles but also many photographs of most European countries, and China, Japan, the USA and Canada - note the sample page shown on page 9 from the hand-written Frith & Co ledgers recording the pictures. By 1890 Frith had created the greatest specialist photographic publishing company in the world, with over 2,000 sales outlets - more than the combined number that Boots and WH Smith have today! The picture on the next page shows the Frith & Co display board at Ingleton in the Yorkshire Dales (left of window). Beautifully constructed with a mahogany frame and gilt inserts, it could display up to a dozen local scenes.

POSTCARD BONANZA

The ever-popular holiday postcard we know today took many years to develop. In 1870 the Post Office issued the first plain cards, with a pre-printed stamp on one face. In 1894 they allowed other publishers' cards to be sent through the mail with an attached adhesive halfpenny stamp. Demand grew rapidly, and in 1895 a new size of postcard was permitted called the court card, but there was little room for illustration. In 1899, a year after Frith's death, a new card measuring 5.5 x 3.5 inches became the standard format, but it was not until 1902 that the divided back came into being, so that the address and message could be on one face and a full-size illustration on the other. Frith & Co were in the vanguard of postcard development: Frith's sons Eustace and Cyril continued their father's monumental task, expanding the number of views offered to the public and recording more and more places

5					
6					
7	St Catherine's College		+		
8	Senate House & Library		+		
30				+	
	Gerrard Hostel Bridge		+	+	+
	Geological Museum				
1	Addenbrooke's Hospital		+		
2	St Mary's Church		+		
3	Fitzwilliam Museum, Pitt Press &c		+		
4			+		
5	Buxton, The Crescent			+	
6	The Colonnade			+	
7	Public Gardens			+	
8				+	
9				+	
40	Haddon Hall, View from the Terrace			+	
	Miller's Dale				

in Britain, as the coasts and countryside were opened up to mass travel.

Francis Frith had died in 1898 at his villa in Cannes, his great project still growing. The archive he created continued in business for another seventy years. By 1970 it contained over a third of a million pictures showing 7,000 British towns and villages.

FRANCIS FRITH'S LEGACY

Frith's legacy to us today is of immense significance and value, for the magnificent archive of evocative photographs he created provides a unique record of change in the cities, towns and villages throughout Britain over a century and more. Frith and his fellow studio photographers revisited locations many times down the years to update their views, compiling for us an enthralling and colourful pageant of British life and character.

We are fortunate that Frith was dedicated to recording the minutiae of everyday life, for it is this sheer wealth of visual data, the painstaking chronicle of changes in dress, transport, street layouts, buildings, housing, engineering and landscape that captivates us so much today. His remarkable images offer us a powerful link with the past and with the lives of our ancestors.

THE VALUE OF THE ARCHIVE TODAY

Computers have now made it possible for Frith's many thousands of images to be accessed almost instantly. Frith's images are increasingly used as visual resources, by social historians, by researchers into genealogy and ancestry, by architects and town planners, and by teachers involved in local history projects.

In addition, the archive offers every one of us an opportunity to examine the places where we and our families have lived and worked down the years. Highly successful in Frith's own era, the archive is now, a century and more on, entering a new phase of popularity. Historians consider the Francis Frith Collection to be of prime national importance. It is the only archive of its kind remaining in private ownership. Francis Frith's archive is now housed in an historic timber barn in the beautiful village of Teffont in Wiltshire. Its founder would not recognize the archive office as it is today. In place of the many thousands of dusty boxes containing glass plate negatives and an all-pervading odour of photographic chemicals, there are now ranks of computer screens. He would be amazed to watch his images travelling round the world at unimaginable speeds through internet lines.

The archive's future is both bright and exciting. Francis Frith, with his unshakeable belief in making photographs available to the greatest number of people, would undoubtedly approve of what is being done today with his lifetime's work. His photographs depicting our shared past are now bringing pleasure and enlightenment to millions around the world a century and more after his death.

OXFORDSHIRE VILLAGES
AN INTRODUCTION

THE SOUTHERN Heart of England county of Oxfordshire boasts a great diversity of scenery and heritage and includes some of the most attractive villages in England. The landscape encompasses the picturesque valleys of the River Thames and its tributaries, the Thame, Cherwell, Windrush and Evenlode; the magnificent steep slopes and beech woods of the Chilterns in the south-east; the rolling hills and dry-stone walls of the Cotswolds in the west and north-west; and the open chalk northern slopes of the Berkshire downs in the south. Throughout the county one will find pleasing and inviting villages set in peaceful farmland or amongst the rolling hills, providing an interesting contrast in their individuality.

The rivers, especially the Thames and Cherwell, have had a great influence on the development of village life in the county ever since the early settlements of the Iron Age. Evidence of these early settlements can be found in various parts of the county, especially near Dorchester, where you can see the Dyke Hills and Castle Hill on Wittenham Clumps. The Romans also settled in the area and built other towns, such as Alchester, near Bicester. The Romans also built major roads, such as Akeman Street, which ran between St Albans and Cirencester, and villas, similar to the one to be found at North Leigh.

During the Saxon period the county was continually being fought over between Wessex in the south and Mercia in the north. The debate as to whether Oxfordshire is a southern county or a Heart of England county still continues to this day. The importance of Dorchester continued to develop, and in the seventh century a Saxon church was built there. During the 12th century a new abbey was built on the site of this early Saxon church. The Domesday Book of 1086 records many small communities that still exist today, including Adderbury, Benson, or Bensington as it was known in those days, and Bampton, which already possessed a market.

A vast medieval forest, the Royal Forest of Wychwood, covered central Oxfordshire, and although clearing began during the Norman era, settlements were still confined to areas near the rivers. During the 13th and 14th centuries, however, clearing started in earnest, and more land was released for agricultural purposes. The low-lying river valleys were eminently suited for agriculture, and many villages began to develop around the farming communities. Oxfordshire is still regarded as one of the best-watered counties in England. The link between farming and river can be found in many of the village and town names. Instances are Appleford, Burford, Heyford, and Oxford; all were medieval river crossings. Oxford grew and flourished over the centuries, and gave the county its current title - Oxfordshire.

The rolling hills of the Cotswolds were favourable for sheep farming, and development took place here during the lucrative wool trade era of the 15th and 16th centuries. The development of agriculture led to the need for markets where farmers could buy and sell their animals and produce. Markets already existed in villages such as Bampton (1086), Burford (1100), Deddington (1190), Adderbury (1218), and Henley-on-Thames (1259). Mainly held in the squares of many of the towns and larger villages, many continued well into the 20th century. Others, including Deddington, succumbed to the competition from the larger towns, such as Banbury. Even though some disappeared, markets still form an essential part of community life in the county today, although competition from modern day supermarkets threatens the survival of the few that still exist. The village squares have survived, however, and market days continue to attract people from far and wide, providing a reminder of their past success.

Geology has played a major part in creating the characteristic diversity that can be found in Oxfordshire's picturesque villages. Geologically, the county can be sub-divided into three principal regions, each one having had an effect on the types of building materials that have been used for the construction of the buildings to be found in the villages. In the south we find the chalk and flint buildings of the Chilterns; in the north it is the quarried marlstone and ironstone that presents a warm orange brown characteristic look; and in the Cotswolds the dominant material is the creamy grey oolitic limestone that gives the buildings their rich golden colour. Up until the mid 19th century, most of the bricks and stone that were used for building was produced locally. Thatch was used on many of the older houses and buildings, and this picturesque roofing material can be seen in villages such as Blewbury, Clifton Hampden, East Hagbourne, and Great Tew.

During the 15th and 16th centuries, houses with cruck trusses were common throughout the area, and examples of these can be found at Deddington, Blewbury, Steventon, and the Great Barn at Coxwell. An alternative to the cruck was the box frame, an elaborate tradition of timber framing that spread from southeast England. Fine examples of these can be found in the villages mentioned above. At Blewbury you can find excellent examples of the gradual invasion of brick, with the infilling of the panels of the timber-framed houses before taking over whole facades.

Many listed buildings and structures can be found throughout the county. Georgian architecture is another prominent feature. Post-war buildings provide contrasting architectural styles to those of the older structures. The county has an interesting variety of churches, many dating back to Saxon and Norman times. In addition to Dorchester Abbey a number of the village churches have fascinating and unusual features. Examples can be found at Bloxham, Barford St Michael, and East Hagbourne. Schools and colleges are another feature of village life, and here again interesting examples can be found at Ewelme, Cuddesdon and Culham. At Ducklington the old village school has been converted into living quarters.

Oxfordshire has some very fine country and manor houses. Excellent examples can be found at Broughton, Chastleton, and Mapledurham, and we must not forget the magnificent Blenheim Palace. Oxfordshire was heavily involved in the 17th-century English Civil War, and Broughton Castle played its part during this period. Viscount Saye and Sele supported the Parliamentarians, and many a meeting was held at this fine manor house. In more recent

times the house has been used as a location in a number of feature films. Sir Winston Churchill, who is buried at the village of Bladon, just to the south of Blenheim Park, was born at Blenheim Palace. The county also had links with a number of well-known literary figures of the past. Garsington, Uffington, Cholsey, Sutton Courtenay, and Blewbury are prime examples, and the author they are connected with can be found in the text that accompanies the village photographs.

By the beginning of the 20th century, Oxfordshire had a good network of roads and railways. It also had the River Thames and the Oxford Canal. The canal, built in 1790, linked Oxford with the Midlands. Brunel's Great Western Railway had arrived in 1841, and Didcot became a major railway centre. A branch line was built to Oxford in 1844, which had been extended to the Midlands by 1852; other links served Thame, Woodstock, and Witney. There was

STEVENTON, *The Causeway c1955* S606009

also a line between Banbury and Cheltenham. The network provided faster and more efficient transfer of wood, stone, coal and agricultural produce to and from the Midlands and other parts of the country, and made commuting to and from the county much easier.

Major industrialisation came to the county in 1912 when William Morris, later Lord Nuffield, produced the first Morris car at his new Morris Motors factory at Cowley. Car production had a great effect on the county, and in addition to its being a centre of learning, Oxford now became an industrial city. It also attracted other related industries, and thus provided urgently needed employment to a county that had been stagnating. The ever-expanding market for cars saw the county prosper even during the economic slump of the 1930s. Other large towns, such as Banbury and Bicester, also attracted small industries. More and more people were moving into the villages, and the demand for accommodation resulted in more and more houses and housing estates being built. Good examples can be seen at Shrivenham, Souldern and South Moreton.

The development of the M40 motorway and other major roads that bypass many of Oxfordshire's villages, have helped to take through traffic away from these rural communities, and thus they have been able to return, to a certain extent, to the peace and tranquillity they so richly deserve. Looking through the photographs in this book, it is amazing how many of them reveal a scene without a motor vehicle in sight - something not easily achieved today. With the opening of the M40 in 1973, Oxfordshire can claim to have the newest motorway and the oldest thoroughfare,

the Ridgeway, running through it.

The last decade or so has seen the demise of many village corner shops, public houses and post offices. These all had a place in traditional village life, and although they still exist in most villages, their characteristics have changed quite significantly. The village shop has become a small mini-market; the village pub, a drinking restaurant; and the post office has either closed, or is part of the village store.

The Francis Frith team visited the area on a number of occasions, and as a result have been able to capture an interesting social record of the county in a fascinating series of photographs that will give the reader a captivating view of what the villages looked like in years gone by. Market squares; picturesque 16th- and 17th-century thatched cottages and houses; old coaching inns; the majestic Thames, or Isis as it is known within Oxfordshire; and the typical English village with duck pond, green, church, post office and corner shop are all displayed in this photographic collection.

For this photographic journey around the villages of Oxfordshire I have sub-divided the book into four specific sections or regions: South Oxfordshire, which includes the Chilterns and the south eastern section of the county; North Oxfordshire, which includes the Cherwell valley and the northern Cotswolds; West Oxfordshire, which includes the Cotswolds; and finally, the Vale of The White Horse, which until 1974 was part of Berkshire. Whatever your thoughts may be on the changes that have taken place, this interesting and fascinating Frith photographic collection provides an opportunity to take a nostalgic look back to a time when life was slower and less stressful than it is today.

SOUTH OXFORDSHIRE

COVERING an area of about 260 square miles, the boundary of South Oxfordshire runs along the borders of Buckinghamshire, Berkshire and the Oxfordshire district of the Vale of the White Horse. Between Henley-on-Thames and Oxford, it follows the course of the River Thames, along which can be found some of Oxfordshire's delightful riverside villages. The landscape is varied and interesting, and includes the western escarpment of the Chilterns. There are fascinating churches here, an abbey, and an old working watermill, which was used as one of the settings in a recent television adaptation of 'Vanity Fair'. The area was also noted for the production of local building stones such as Wheatley, Haseley and Milton, all named after the villages where they were produced.

SHIPLAKE
The Church 1890
27172

Shiplake parish church was originally built in the 12th century. It was here, in 1850, that the poet Alfred Lord Tennyson married Emily Sellwood. The church also has some medieval stained glass, thought to have come from a ruined abbey in France.

SHIPLAKE
Below the Lock 1890
27165

The lock gate is open in readiness for the arrival or departure of some river craft. It is not known for certain whether the house on the island served refreshments in 1890, but today it is a favourite stopping off place, where both river users and walkers can spend a lazy hour or so enjoying afternoon tea.

MAPLEDURHAM, *The Mill and the Church 1890* 27092

Originally built in the 16th century, the mill, situated in the grounds of Mapledurham House, has been lovingly restored and today provides a fine example of a working Thames watermill. Visitors can purchase the wholemeal flour that is produced there. The tower of the church can just be seen behind the mill.

MAPLEDURHAM *from the air 1972* AFA231134

▼ **MAPLEDURHAM,** *The Church 1910* 62214

The idyllic setting of St Margaret's Church provides the resting place of Sir Richard Blount, whose tomb can be found in the churchyard. Mapledurham House was built for him and his family during the 16th century. The clock on the 13th-century church tower bears the initials of King William IV, who presented it as a gift in 1832.

► **MAPLEDURHAM**
Mapledurham House c1955 M25013

Here we see a small section of Mapledurham House, one of the largest Elizabethan houses in Oxfordshire. The house still has an original 16th century ceiling. If you look carefully, you may just see an inquisitive dog looking out of the central window. Was it trying to escape, or did it simply want to be in the photograph?

◄ **MAPLEDURHAM**
The Lock 1917
67970A

The 'River Queen' is leaving Mapledurham Lock. The river vessel has a full complement of passengers, and it looks as if they had a pleasant fine day for their outing. Typical early 20th-century fashions can be seen on those standing and sitting on the bank of the Thames.

► **MAPLEDURHAM**
The Mill House
c1955 M25018

The name Mapledurham is thought to derive from an old Saxon word, Mapledreham, which means 'a homestead by the maple tree'. The Mill House is the large house with the three attic windows. The building, with the wooden fence on the left is part of what was once Mapledurham's post office.

► **MOULSFORD**
The Church 1890
27031

Here we see the
quaint 12th-century
riverside church
with its wooden
bellcot in the village
of Moulsford. The
village is also noted
for its picturesque
riverside inn known
as the Beetle and
Wedge. The 'beetle'
in this instance refers
to a heavy-headed
hammer, and not to
an insect.

◄ **NETTLEBED**
High Street c1955
N79021

This view of the High
Street was taken from the
Cookley/Watlington road
junction. Nettlebed was
once a very important
brick and tile-making
centre in the area, and
one of the old kilns still
remains in the village.
A close-up of the High
Street can be seen in
photograph N79010.

▲ **NETTLEBED,** *The Bull Hotel and the High Street c1955* N79010

A sign on the wall of the Bull Hotel, seen on the left, informs passers-by that 'you may telephone from here'. Next to the hotel is the Nettlebed Stores, where a bicycle is propped up near the entrance. On the opposite side of the road a car is just pulling away from the garage of H P Davies. Just beyond the garage is the White Hart Hotel.

◄ **NETTLEBED**
The White Hart Hotel
c1955 N79012

This charming red brick building is located in the High Street, in the centre of the village. It is an excellent example, and reminder, of Nettlebed's important brick-making days, which dated back to the 14th century. It is reputed that Queen Elizabeth I once stayed at the White Hart Hotel, which gives some indication of its age.

SOUTH STOKE
The Church 1898
42562

St Andrew's Church stands on the route of the ancient thoroughfare, the Ridgeway. The church incorporates several periods of architecture, the oldest being Early English; the font dates from the 14th century. The chancel contains a memorial dedicated to Griffith Higgs, who became chaplain to King Charles I, and then to his sister when she became Queen of Bohemia.

NORTH STOKE, *The Church 1898* 42563

Inside St Mary's Church, built in the 13th century, there is a Jacobean font and some interesting wall paintings. If you visit the churchyard today, you should find amongst the gravestones near the west side of the tower a memorial to the singer Dame Clara Butt, who once lived in the village.

CHOLSEY
Wallingford Road c1960 C289001

The road sign, in the centre of the photograph, indicates that the Wallingford road turns to the right just beyond the houses on the right. F Williams's shop on the extreme right displays a board advertising Zebo – a grate blackener. If you were to continue directly ahead you would arrive at St Mary's Church, where the author Agatha Christie is buried.

EWELME, *The School c1965* E59028

The Duke of Suffolk and his wife Alice, granddaughter of the poet Geoffrey Chaucer, built the two-storey primary school in the mid 1400s. The school, which is still in use today, is one of the oldest active schools in the county. Behind the school are some almshouses, seen in photograph E59015 (page 24), that were built during the same period.

▲ **EWELME**
The Almshouses, the Arcade c1950
E59015

When the almshouses were built in 1437 there were originally thirteen. Recent modernisation, however, has seen the number reduced to eight - the other five have been re-located to the main street. In the photograph, an old pump wheel can be seen in the quadrangle.

▶ *detail from* E59015

EWELME
The Chapel of the Almsmen c1950
E59013

The church, which dates from the same period as the school and almshouses, also has a magnificent ten-foot high 15th-century wooden font. The grave of Jerome K Jerome, author of 'Three Men in a Boat', can be found in the churchyard.

BENSON, *Bensington Weir 1893* 31704

Benson's original name was Bensington, which means 'Bensa's Farm'. For centuries the River Thames played a major role in Benson's history. Until the mid 1930s, coal was transported from the Midlands via the Oxford Canal to Oxford, and thence along the Thames to Benson, where it was offloaded.

▶ **BENSON**
The Riverside Café
c1950 B364010

Many a traveller, either
using the Thames or
perhaps simply walking
by, may well remember
using the Riverside Café.
When this photograph was
taken the sexes were well
segregated if they wanted
to use the toilet; the ladies
went to the left of the
building, and the gents went
to the right.

◄ **BENSON**
The Post Office c1950
B364021

The post office can be seen in the right centre of the photograph. Just beyond the shop is the Crown, indicated by the crown on the pub sign, which is RAC approved. The village started growing during the turnpike era, and stagecoaches stopped at some of the local hostelries on their way between London and Oxford.

◄ *(far left) detail from*
B364021

► **BENSON**
The High Street c1960 B364047

With RAF Benson located nearby, the village has played an important role for the service personnel stationed there. In this photograph, the lady with the pram, on the left, is standing outside the premises of A C Lester & Son Ltd. Their delivery van is parked at the roadside – is it ready for action? Perhaps not, considering that it is parked on the pavement.

◄ **WARBOROUGH**
The Post Office c1955 W252001

The post office, situated in this pretty black and white cottage, opened in 1840, the year the Penny Black stamp first appeared. The position of sub-postmaster remained in the same family until the post office closed in 1987. The last incumbent, Thomas King, served for 41 years; his long spell of duty is commemorated by a plaque on the garden wall.

▲ **WARBOROUGH,** *The Village Pump c1955* W252009

In the days of not so long ago, the village pump provided the main water supply for its residents. As we can see here, the village pump at Warborough has been well preserved. Its open wooden gazebo-type covering helped to keep the villagers relatively dry whilst they filled their buckets and containers.

◀ **WARBOROUGH**
The Green c1960
W252018

Football and cricket are played on the large village green throughout the year. Local records indicate that cricket has been played there for over 130 years. Where do the players go after the game? One possible answer can be seen in photograph W252020, page 30!

WARBOROUGH
The Cricketers c1960
W252020

The Cricketers overlooks the village green in Warborough, and thus it is the most convenient pub for all the thirsty sporting fraternity. The village has other hostelries to choose from if the Cricketers is full, including the Six Bells and the Kingfisher.

SHILLINGFORD, *The Bridge 1893* 31702

The hamlet of Shillingford joins with the village of Warborough, seen in the previous photographs. The three-arched Shillingford Bridge, which carries the Wallingford road over the Thames, was built in 1827. The Shillingford Hotel can be seen on the other side of the river.

▲ **DORCHESTER**
The Abbey 1890 27016

The Abbey Church of St Peter and St
Paul occupies the site of an Augustinian
abbey, which had been erected in 1140
to replace an earlier Saxon church.
Originally a Roman town, Dorchester
became a centre of Christianity in AD635.
Note the unusual wicker basket-type
carriage with a toddler on board with the
young children on the left.

◀ *detail from* 27016

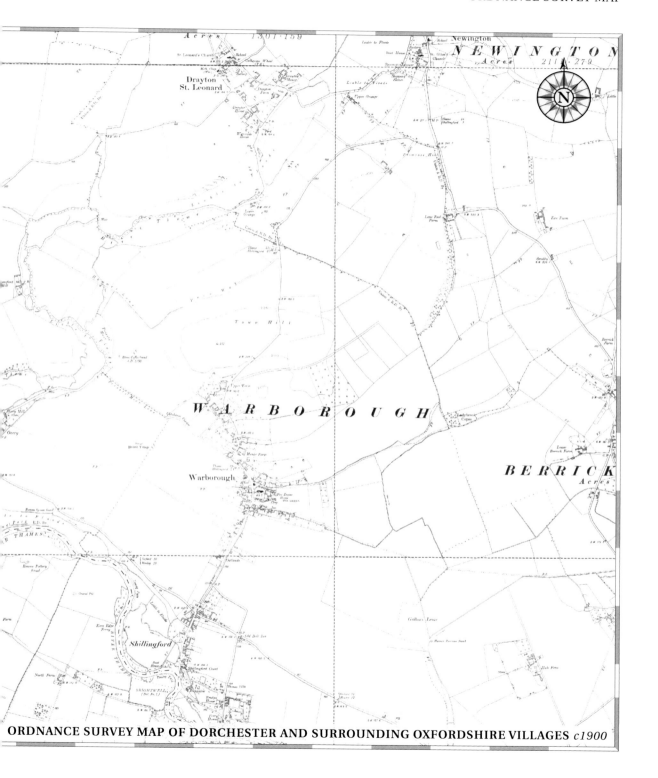

ORDNANCE SURVEY MAP OF DORCHESTER AND SURROUNDING OXFORDSHIRE VILLAGES *c1900*

▼ **DORCHESTER,** *The Abbey, the East Window 1924* 76214

The view looking towards the great east window has changed very little since this photograph was taken. The panelling in front of the choir stalls has changed, so that there is now a more open view. To the right (south) of the chancel is the Lady Chapel, which holds the shrine of St Birinus, the founder of the original Saxon cathedral.

► **DORCHESTER**
The Village c1955
D82008

The road through the village became one of the first turnpike roads in Oxfordshire. As a result, Dorchester ended up with a number of coaching inns, including the 16th-century Fleur De Lys Inn, seen on the left in the photograph. The houses in the village are rich in architectural design, and provide much interest to visitors.

CLIFTON HAMPDEN
The Bridge 1890
27007

The six-arched bridge, designed by Sir George Gilbert Scott, was built in 1864 using bricks made locally. During the same period he also rebuilt the church, which had become derelict. It is reported that in 1862, after a visit to Oxford, the Lord Mayor of London's State Barge ran aground here.

CLIFTON HAMPDEN
From the Meadows 1890 27009

The spire of the church of St Michael and All Angels can just be seen towering above the trees on the far side of the meadow. Near the church porch there is a stone marking the grave of William Dyke. He is reputed to have started the Battle of Waterloo when he accidentally fired his musket.

CLIFTON HAMPDEN
The Village c1955
C121007

The village has some delightful thatched cottages, as we can see here. Further down the hill, the building with a telephone kiosk nearby is Clifton Hampden's post office. The red telephone kiosk is unique – it is a listed building.

▼ **NUNEHAM COURTENAY,** *The Bridge c1881* 13785

The planned estate village of Nuneham Courtenay was created for Simon Courtenay, the first Earl of Harcourt in 1760. Cottages in the village are laid out in pairs and have an identical design of chequered bricks, similar to the charming example we can see in the photograph.

► **NUNEHAM COURTENAY**
From the Bridge 1890
26976

The bridge from where the photograph was taken crosses a little inlet that leads off the main River Thames. Here we see a family feeding the swans whilst they are moored on the bank of the inlet in Nuneham Park, parts of which were landscaped by Capability Brown.

◄ **NUNEHAM COURTENAY**
The Carfax Monument 1890
26979

Standing on the hill overlooking Nuneham Park, the monument is better known today as the Carfax Conduit. It originally stood in the middle of the Carfax junction in Oxford, where its major role was to convey piped water into the city from the Hinksey reservoir.

► **CHISLEHAMPTON**
Chislehampton House c1960 C728022

Sir Charles Peers, at one time Lord Mayor of London, built Chislehampton House in the mid 1760s. The elegant manor house was constructed using bricks made locally. The name Chislehampton is derived from the words 'cisel' and 'hampton', which translate as 'a grave in a high enclosure'.

▶ **CHISLEHAMPTON**
The Village c1960
C728025

Here we see the B480 as it passes through the village; we are looking towards Oxford. The Coach and Horses pub can be seen on the right. The photographer is standing at the northern end of the fine Tudor bridge that crosses the River Thames. In 1643 Prince Rupert and his troops crossed here on the way to his victorious battle at Chalgrove.

◀ **STADHAMPTON**
The Coach and Horses c1955 S782004

Situated 7 miles from the centre of Oxford, the 16th-century Coach and Horses is an old coaching inn, as its name suggests. The inn, which provides accommodation, is reputed to be haunted by a young girl who was killed during the English Civil War.

▲ **STADHAMPTON,** *The Hunt Stables c1955* S782010

During the 19th century the village was home to the Old Berkshire Hunt, and later to the South Oxfordshire Hunt, when new kennels were built. The hunting days have long since gone, and today you are more likely to find an Oxfordshire Animal Sanctuary here.

◄ **STADHAMPTON**
The Village c1960
S782016

The village of Stadhampton is not recorded in the Domesday Book; the first records of its name appear in the mid 12th century. A number of Georgian and thatched properties, similar to the one seen here, can still be found in parts of the village. The oldest building is said to be Doyleys Farmhouse.

► **STADHAMPTON**
The Village c1960
S782024

For many years the green in Stadhampton was home to an annual fair known as the Stadham Feast. The owner of the thatched house on the right of the photograph was obviously interested in topiary, as he has a tree with an interesting circular design in his garden.

SANDFORD-ON-THAMES
The Lock c1955 S348009

Sandford has the deepest lock on the Thames with a drop of 8 feet 10 inches. It is 174 feet long and 21 feet 9 inches wide, and opened in 1914. It is a popular stopping-off point for both river users and walkers in order to sample the refreshments at the King's Arms Hotel.

▼ **SANDFORD-ON-THAMES**
The River and the Kings Arms Hotel c1955 S348004

Sandford Mill, originally built by the Knights Templar in the 13th century, once ground corn. It became a paper mill producing paper for Oxford University. Rags needed for the production of paper were brought by barge from London. Having closed in the 1970s, it has since been demolished and replaced by attractive riverside apartments.

► **SANDFORD-ON-THAMES**
The Main Road c1955
S348010

This photograph shows the main road running through Sandford. Today the A4074 bypasses the village, so the old road tends to retain the more peaceful atmosphere we sense here. A notice just to the left of the nearest telegraph pole advertises the Royal Show in Oxford, scheduled for the 4th to the 7th of July.

◄ **GARSINGTON**
The Village c1960
G335009

Garsington derives its name from the Anglo Saxon 'gaerse dun', which means 'grassy hill'. Passing through the village in 1960, one may well have stopped at the garage and general store in Clinkards Hill to purchase a Walls ice cream or to fill up with Shell petrol from the old hand pumps.

► **GARSINGTON**
The Village c1955
G335002

The older generation may remember visiting Wheeler's, the grocer's and confectioner's, seen on the left in this photograph. The village still has a medieval stone cross, which is thought to date back to 1240. The proximity of the Oxford motor industry made Garsington an ideal place to live for those who came to work there.

▶ **GARSINGTON**
*The Manor House
c1955* G335007

The Manor House was built about 1625 on the site of a previous building. After the First World War the owner at that time, Lady Ottoline Morrell, entertained many famous writers and artists there, including Bertrand Russell and D H Lawrence, and also Virginia Woolf and other members of the Bloomsbury Group.

◀ **CUDDESDON**
High Street c1960
C292007

Once the official home of the Bishops of Oxford for over 400 years, the village earned its title as Oxfordshire's 'Holy Village'. Bishop Samuel Wilberforce founded a theological school, Ripon College, here in 1853. The old Bat and Ball coaching inn, seen on the right, boasts a large selection of cricket memorabilia.

▲ **CUDDESDON,** *Denton Hill c1965* C292017

This scene, looking up Denton Hill towards Cuddesdon, has not changed much to this day. The shop is no longer there, however. Behind the hedge on the right are some playing fields. The road leads into the High Street at the top of the hill.

◄ **CUDDESDON**
The Old Mill and the River c1955 C292021

A swan glides gracefully on the water of the River Thames. In the background we see the old mill, which today lies derelict. It is situated approximately half a mile to the east of the village, and in its day would have provided flour for the bishops and parishioners.

LITTLE MILTON
The Green c1955
L185002

The attractive thatched cottage, seen in the centre of the photograph, houses the village post office. Today the entrance has moved to the right, where we can just see a pram and a dog. An estate agent currently occupies the left section of the building. Many of the buildings in the village date from the 15th to the 17th centuries.

GREAT HASELEY
The Village c1955
G129010

Considerable building work took place in Great Haseley during the 1700s, including the building housing the Crown Inn, seen to the centre left with the pub sign. The inn has since closed, and it is now a private dwelling house. The village also has a Grade I listed tithe barn.

GREAT HASELEY, *The Post Office c1955* G129013

The village post office and stores, seen here in Rectory Road, has closed since the time this photograph was taken. The proprietors have placed a convenient bench seat outside, where customers can rest and eat their Walls ice cream. It must have been popular, because there are three boards advertising the product.

LITTLE HASELEY
The Village c1960
L543015

Little Haseley, as its name suggests, is the smaller of the Haseley villages, and is situated to the south of Great Haseley; this photograph shows a view of the village looking north towards its larger brother. Its crowning glory is possibly Haseley Court, seen in photograph L543016.

LITTLE HASELEY, *Haseley Court c1960* L543016

The statues at the top of the steps leading up to the house are cherubs playing with lions. A hoop on the lawn indicates that croquet was played there. Haseley Court has a splendid topiary garden, which is well worth seeing. In addition this fine medieval house has a 15th-century barn on the estate.

NORTH OXFORDSHIRE AND THE CHERWELL VALLEY

ALL THE VILLAGES in this section are situated in the area of Oxfordshire that lies to the north and north east of Oxford. To the east of the county boundary lie Buckinghamshire and Northamptonshire, and in the north Oxfordshire borders on Warwickshire. Most of the southern part of this area lies within the great Oxfordshire plains, the Cherwell valley and Otmoor. As one heads north the terrain becomes more undulating and the villages take on a totally different character, with the dark brown and tawny orange marlstone buildings contrasting with the light stone of the northern Cotswolds. Many of the villages developed and grew with the trade that used the Oxford Canal. It remains very much an agricultural area.

LOWER HEYFORD
The Long Bridge c1955 L188013

Until the mid 13th century the village was known as Heyford, a ford at which farmers could bring their hay across the River Cherwell. After the bridge was built it became known as Heyford Bridge. The names Heyford Purcell and Nether Heyford were used prior to its taking on its current name of Lower Heyford.

▶ **LOWER HEYFORD**
*Station Road
c1955* L188002

Lower Heyford was one of the original stations on the Oxford to Banbury branch of the Great Western Railway when it opened in 1850. The railway runs very close to the Oxford Canal, and as we can see in photograph L188013, page 51, the River Cherwell is not far away.

◀ **LOWER HEYFORD**
Station Road c1965
L188316

Here we have another view of Station Road, with the Red Lion inn on the right. The inn no longer exists. On the outskirts of Lower Heyford is Rousham House. Built for the Dormer family in the 17th century, its gardens were landscaped by William Kent in the 18th century. Both Lower and Upper Heyford lie within the Rousham Conservation Area.

▲ **LOWER HEYFORD,** *Freehold Street c1955* H233008

Here we are looking down Freehold Street with its old ironstone cottages. At the bottom of the road there is a small square where you will find the Bell Inn, which dates from 1602. A road leads off to the right before you reach the inn; this leads to the Oxford Canal.

◄ **STEEPLE ASTON**
The Church c1955
S354003

St Peter's Church, seen here, has never had a steeple. In this particular instance, the word steeple derives from the the 13th-century word 'stepel', meaning an unfortified tower. Inside the church there are some white marble effigies of Sir Francis and Lady Page. The former was known as a 'hanging judge', having sentenced over 100 men to death during his lifetime.

▲ **STEEPLE ASTON**
The Village c1955 S354006

Two men and a young boy are rummaging at the back of a horse and cart in North Side. Another young lad, standing in the middle of the road, looks on with great interest. The area around Steeple Aston contains over 30 listed buildings.

► *detail from* S354006

STEEPLE ASTON
South Street c1955
S354017

Here we have a view looking along South Street. The old post office can be seen on the left, and just further along is the White Lion inn. On the outskirts of the village there is a folly known as the Rousham Eyecatcher; it was designed by William Kent, who landscaped Rousham House in Lower Heyford.

SOULDERN, *Bovewell c1965* S352002

Bovewell is situated on the eastern edge of the village. When this photograph was taken the small estate looked fairly new, and the front gardens are neat and well maintained. Open fields can be seen in the background. In earlier days Souldern was known as Sulthorn because of the many thorn trees that grew in the area.

▼ **SOULDERN,** *High Street c1965* S352005

On the left is Souldern's post office, which, according to one of the signs outside the shop, was part of the premises of M Lee & Son, a family grocer who also sold beers, wines and spirits. The street was quite pretty at this time of year - the plants on the houses beyond the post office appear to be in flower.

► **DEDDINGTON**
The Village c1950
D107008

Looking up Philcote Street we see the tower of the 13th-century church of St Peter and St Paul. It once had a steeple, but this collapsed in the 17th century and was never rebuilt. Many of the old houses in the village are built with Horton stone, giving them a light golden tint.

DEDDINGTON
Market Square
c1950 D107016

An old bus is seen passing the northern extremity of the Market Square, possibly on its way to Banbury. The deserted square makes it difficult to imagine that Deddington was once a very prosperous agricultural centre. At its annual Pudding and Pie fair, 600 or more horses would be sold.

DEDDINGTON
Market Square
c1960 D107032

Here we see a view of the southern end of the Market Square. On the far side of the square we can see the Unicorn Hotel, and to its left, where a car is parked, is the Corner Café. Just out of picture, on the right, is the Town Hall, which once housed a couple of old hand-operated fire engines.

▶ **BARFORD ST MICHAEL**
Rock Cottage and Turnstile House c1960 B362002

The 1960s were an important period in the history of Barford St Michael. The arrival of mains drainage, thus alleviating the use of septic tanks and cesspits, saw the village grow quite significantly, with new houses and cottages blending with the old.

◀ **BARFORD ST MICHAEL**
The Village c1960 B362005

The buildings on the right provide an interesting example of the old blending with the new. A modern house, or extension, has been built next to an old thatched cottage. The 12th-century church of St Michael, in the village, has a porch that is decorated with Norman beak-heads, representing the faces of wild animals.

▲ **BARFORD ST MICHAEL,** *Lower Street c1960* B362012

These twin thatched cottages are fine examples of some of the interesting old houses to be found in Lower Street. The George Inn, out of shot, is another thatched 2-storey building, dating from 1672. Many of the older houses to be found in this part of North Oxfordshire are built using ironstone.

◄ **BLOXHAM**
The Village c1960
B367018

We are looking along the High Street towards St Mary's Church. A solitary van stands outside the premises of an antique shop called The Bloxham Gallery. The spire of the church, reputed to have been commissioned by Cardinal Wolsey, towers to a height of 198 feet. It can be seen from miles around.

BLOXHAM
Little Bridge Road
c1960 B367020

Little Bridge Road leads off the High Street. Today it would take you down to some playing fields. Built to house workers in the ironstone industry, which was mined locally, many of the buildings date from the period when that industry was at its height. The village also accommodates many families who work in Banbury, just 3½ miles away.

► **BLOXHAM**
All Saints' School
c1955 B367010

Some young lads take time out from lessons to play cricket on the sports field of Bloxham School. The boy on the left obviously means business, rolling up his sleeve as he prepares to bowl to the boy on the right, who waits patiently, bat in hand. It appears, however, that the bowler has no wickets to bowl at.

◄ **ADDERBURY**
Oxford Road c1955
A139008

The offices of Leonard Hickham, seen on the left in the photograph, replaced the Wheatsheaf public house, indicated by the old inn sign. Further along is the Red Lion. This is the oldest inn in Adderbury, and dates back to the 16th century. It still has its original oak beams and large stone fireplaces.

▲ **ADDERBURY,** *West Adderbury from Milton Road c1955* A139014

Adderbury has origins dating back to Saxon times. It prospered and grew during the productive era of the wool trade. Its honey-coloured stone cottages, with their floral gardens, have led to it winning the Best Kept Village on a number of occasions.

◄ **BROUGHTON**
The Church 1921 70596

The Church of St Mary, with its imposing tower and spire, mainly dates from the 14th century. Inside there is an elaborate painted tomb where Sir John de Broughton is buried. The fortified manor house, Broughton Castle, which is seen in photograph 72107 on pages 68 and 69, was built for him during the early part of the 14th century.

BROUGHTON
The Saye and Sele Arms 1922 72116

An early model motor car is seen driving past the Saye and Sele Arms advertising Brackley Ales and Stout. The inn takes its name from nearby Broughton Castle, the ancestral home of the Lords Saye and Sele. The twin title has its origins dating back to the mid 15th century.

▶ **BROUGHTON**
The Castle 1922 72107

William Fiennes, the 2nd Lord Saye and Sele, acquired Broughton Castle through marriage during the 15th century. It has remained with the family ever since. The photograph shows a good view of the manor house (the castle), the gatehouse and the church spire; we are looking across the moat from Broughton Park.

◄ **BROUGHTON**
The Castle and the Gatehouse 1922 72114

The photograph shows a close up view of the gatehouse, a feature that was added to give the manor a more castellated appearance. Broughton Castle has been used in more modern times as the location for a number of films, including 'Shakespeare in Love', made in 1998. In the film it was the stately home of Viola.

◄ *(far left) detail from* 72114

► **CROPREDY**
The Village c1960
C291020

Although Cropredy (pronounced Cropreedy) has grown and has been modernised, the old ironstone cottages still manage to retain their charm. The village became well known during the English Civil War when a major battle to control Cropredy Bridge was fought here in June 1644. Today, on an August weekend, the village plays host to a music festival organised by the folk-rock group Fairport Convention.

◄ **CROPREDY**
Red Lion Street and the Parish Church c1955
C291005

The very narrow Red Lion Street in Cropredy is named after the Red Lion Inn, seen half way along the row of houses on the right. The lectern in the 11th-century church of St Mary the Virgin was damaged during the Civil War. It was incorrectly repaired, and now has two brass feet and one bronze.

◄ *(far left) detail from*
C291005

CROPREDY
The Brasenose Inn
c1955 C291009

The Brasenose Inn obtained its name from the fact that it was built on land owned by Brasenose College, Oxford. During the summer it is very popular with walkers and with members of the boating fraternity who use the Oxford Canal. At one time, Cropredy had two wharves on the canal.

HORLEY, *The Church c1955* H234005

The tower and chancel are all that remain of the original Norman church of St Etheldreda. The rest of the church has been rebuilt or restored at some time or other over the centuries. It also has an interesting sun dial, which we can see at the top left of the photograph.

HORLEY, *The Mural of St Christopher in the Church c1955* H234007

This magnificent wall painting of St Christopher holding the infant Jesus is thought to date from c1450. Painted on the north wall of the church, it was described by Pevsner as being 'one of the most perfect, and largest, representations of the saint in the country.'

THE OXFORDSHIRE COTSWOLDS

THIS REGION, stretching from the Thames, west of Oxford, to the Warwickshire boundary in the north, provides some of the best scenic countryside to be found in Oxfordshire. Here we find the market towns of Burford and Chipping Norton, both owing their early prosperity to sheep farming; Witney, once renowned for its blankets; and Woodstock and Bladon, both situated at the edge of Blenheim Park. Attractive villages, including that crème de la crème of estate villages, Great Tew, are to be found nestling in the valleys of the eastern Cotswolds. Bampton is noted for its Morris dancing, and although the traditional Horse Fair has gone, the dancers can still be seen dancing through the streets during the summer months.

SALFORD, *The Village c1965* S781002

Situated a couple of miles to the west of Chipping Norton, the village of Salford is thought to derive its name from the fact that it may have a been a stopping-off point along the route of the Salt Way that ran from Droitwich to the south coast.

GREAT TEW
The Post Office
c1960 G130018

Surrounded by rolling hills, this has to be one of the most beautiful villages in Oxfordshire. J C Loudon, author of 'The Encyclopedia of Cottage, Farm and Villa Architecture and Furniture', inspired its design as an estate village in the 19th century. Golden ironstone cottages topped with thatch and shady trees make it the perfect idyll.

GREAT TEW, *The Village c1955* G130002

Thatched cottages, similar to those shown in the photograph, attract a great number of visitors to the village. The village is also associated with Viscount Falkland, who inherited the manor of Great Tew during the 17th century. He became Secretary of State to Charles I.

▼ **GREAT TEW,** *The Village c1960* G130014

A young girl looks down a quiet country lane in the village of Great Tew. Perhaps she is waiting for her father to come home from a nearby farm. Her mother looks down pensively at her young daughter. The scene captures the idyllic peace and tranquillity that this delightful village conveys to its many visitors.

► **TACKLEY**
The Green c1965
T146008

Amongst the houses on the left of the large triangular village green is the family grocer's run by M Broome. As is the case with many village shops, it has now closed. Tackley grew quite considerably after the Second World War due to the fact that many workers at the Cowley car works in Oxford came to live here.

◄ **TACKLEY**
Nethercote Road
c1965 T146009

In the centre of
the picture is the
King's Arms pub in
Nethercote Road. The
road leads to Tackley
Station, which is on
the main Oxford to
Banbury line. Most
of the thatch on the
older cottages has
been replaced by
slate today.

► **TACKLEY**
The School c1965
T146012

Tackley CE Primary
School, in St John's
Road, can be seen
on the left in the
photograph. The
young lad walking
beside his mother on
the pavement, looks
too young to attend
school. Perhaps his
mother has been
showing him where he
may soon be starting
his education. Perhaps
one day he may be an
expert on the history
of Oxfordshire villages.

▲ **BLADON**
*Sir Winston Churchill's Grave
c1965* B366018

▶ **BLADON**
St Martin's Church c1965
B366016

A queue of people line up to
pay their respects to Sir Winston
Churchill, who was buried in the
churchyard of St Martin's Church on
30 January 1965. The photograph
must have been taken soon after
his interment there. His wife
Clementine was buried here in
1977. The family plot also contains
the graves of Randolph and Jennie
Churchill, the parents of Sir Winston.
A close-up view of the grave can be
seen in photograph B366018, above.

◄ **BLADON**
Park Street c1960
B366009

The photograph shows a view of Park Street looking towards Woodstock. This is the main A4095 road that runs through the village. A small Esso petrol station can just be seen on the left, just where the road bends to the right.

◄ **BLADON**
The White House c1960 B366011

Situated on the corner of Park Street and Park Lane, which leads into Blenheim Park, is the White House inn. Its main supplier of beers and ales in those days was Ind Coope. The inn has been modernised and updated since this photograph was taken.

SHORTHAMPTON
The Church c1955
S830013

All Saints' Church, Shorthampton, was originally built during the 12th century, but was added to and partially rebuilt during the 15th century. Inside there are traces of wall paintings depicting scenes from the Bible. The church stands on a hilltop looking out over the Evenlode valley.

ASCOTT-UNDER-WYCHWOOD, *The Swan c1950* A140008

The Swan, seen on the left, is now the only remaining pub in Ascott-under-Wychwood. The pub acts as the village post office on Monday mornings. Ascott is actually divided into two areas. The east end is called Ascott d'Oyley, and the west side is called Ascott Earl.

SHIPTON-UNDER-WYCHWOOD
The Green c1955
S349003

The fountain and memorial, seen to the right of the tree, were erected in memory of seventeen parishioners who perished during their voyage to New Zealand. Their ship, the 'Cospatrick', caught fire near the island of Tristan da Cunha in November 1874.

SHIPTON-UNDER-WYCHWOOD, *The Church c1955* S349009

The Church of St Mary, with its tall stone spire, is thought to date from the 12th century. Shipton was an important royal manor in Saxon times, and there was probably a minster church on the site during that period. The Forest of Wychwood was a favourite hunting ground for monarchs up to the Tudor era.

► **MINSTER LOVELL**
*The Manor House
Ruins c1955* M161002

Behind the ruins of Minster
Lovell Hall, seen in the
foreground, is St Kenelm's
Church. William Lovell
built the church and rebuilt
the Hall during the 15th
century. The Domesday
Book records a hall being
on the site at the time of the
survey. Inside the church,
which is named after a
Saxon prince (Kenelm),
there is an effigy of William
Lovell.

► *(far right) detail from*
M161002

◄ DUCKLINGTON
The Village c1950
D110007

A solitary young lad is seen carrying what could be an old bicycle tyre – or could it be a hula-hoop? Ducklington is renowned for the fact that a rare plant, the snakeshead fritillary, grows in a field near the church. Its flowering is celebrated annually on Fritillary Sunday.

◄ *(far right) detail from*
D110007

DUCKLINGTON
The Pond c1965
D110058

Behind the village pond, which is still there today, is the Old School building. Note the school bell-cote on the roof. Although the building, which dates from 1849, has now been converted into a private dwelling house, it still retains its character, complete with bell-cote.

▶ **BAMPTON**
Bridge Street c1965
B363001

The photograph shows a view of Bridge Street looking towards the town centre. On the left, just beyond the chapel, is the old Wheatsheaf Inn. Bampton, with its interesting variety of 17th- and 18th-century buildings, has strong traditional links with Morris dancing.

◀ **BAMPTON**
The Memorial c1965
B363013

The war memorial is situated in the Market Square. Out of picture to its left is Bampton Town Hall, which was built in 1838 by George Wilkinson. The building to the right of the cross is the old Jubilee Inn. The Domesday Book survey records that Bampton already had a market operating at this time.

▲ **BAMPTON,** *St Mary's Church c1965* B363033

St Mary's Church, one of the largest churches in Oxfordshire, has a 170ft spire. Originally Norman, it is built on the site of a Saxon minster. Changes were made to the building during the 13th and 14th centuries, which is when the flying buttresses were added.

◀ **RADCOT**
*The River Thames
c1960* R414040

A tranquil River Thames flows under Radcot Bridge, a section of which can be seen on the left in the photograph. The triple-arched structure is the oldest surviving bridge on the Thames. Built in the 12th century, it is thought to have Saxon foundations. Stone from nearby quarries was carried to London by barge and used in the building of St Paul's Cathedral.

THE VALE OF THE WHITE HORSE

FOR CENTURIES the southern border of Oxfordshire was formed by the River Thames, then in 1974 a major change took place when the Boundaries Commission ruled that the area north of the Berkshire Downs, known as the Vale of The White Horse, should be transferred from Berkshire to Oxfordshire. Covering an area stretching from the edge of Oxford to the borders of Wiltshire and Gloucestershire in the west, and from the River Thames to the Berkshire Downs in the south, the undulating beauty of the Vale of the White Horse with its enchanting landscape provides an excellent finale to this fascinating insight into some of Oxfordshire's oldest and most picturesque villages.

SHRIVENHAM, *Downsview Estate c1965* S350030

Shrivenham, nestling on the Wiltshire border, is one of the most westerly villages in the Vale of the White Horse. The Downsview Estate was fairly new when this photograph was taken. As its name suggests, there are some good views looking south towards the Berkshire Downs.

WATCHFIELD
A Pretty Cottage and the Church c1960
W253021

The church, and this pretty thatched cottage, present quite a contrast to the buildings of the Royal Military College of Science that stand elsewhere in the village. Modern development has almost linked Watchfield with the village of Shrivenham. In earlier days they were both part of the ancient manor of Beckett.

WOOLSTONE, *The Village c1960* W634005

Woolstone has a number of cottages dating from the 17th century, many with thatch similar to the one seen in the photograph. Situated in the valley below the chalk figure of the White Horse, the village has a spring with water that tastes as good as if not better than the piped water of today.

▶ **WOOLSTONE**
The White Horse Inn c1960 W634006

The White Horse Inn is thought to date from the 16th century. The inn has not changed much to this day, but the sign and railings have gone and the frontage is not so open. Stables to the right of the inn have been converted, and provide additional accommodation.

◀ **UFFINGTON**
Broad Street c1960 U24010

The building on the left houses the village post office. Advertising signs on the wall indicates that it sells Lyons tea and Lyons cakes. It is interesting to speculate what the man standing on the box is doing. He has no paint pot or bucket, but he does have some object in his hand – is he puttying the window?

▲ **UFFINGTON,** *The Village Store c1960* U24012

This delightful thatched cottage housed the village store, which at the time the photograph was taken was run by P Burgess. As a family grocer, he provided groceries and provisions, including Lyons cakes and ice cream. It seems that no one went hungry in Uffington during the 1960s.

◄ **UFFINGTON**
The Village c1960
U24019

The thatched building in the centre of the photograph housed the Baker's Arms public house, which sold Morland's beers. The only pub in the village today is the Fox and Hounds. Thomas Hughes, author of 'Tom Brown's Schooldays', was born in Uffington.

▼ **UFFINGTON,** *Thatched Cottage c1960* U24024

It is possible that thatched cottages similar to the one seen here provided the attraction that brought Sir John Betjeman to set up home in the village. Those were the days when one could leave a bicycle standing against a wooden fence without much fear of someone running off with it. It does seem a strange place to leave it, though.

▶ **BUCKLAND**
The Trout Inn c1965
B368004

Situated on Buckland Marsh near Tadpole Bridge, about one and a half miles from the main village, the inn is very popular with those walking the Thames Path National Trail. One of its former landlords was reputed to have had the name A Herring - most appropriate for a riverside hostelry!

◄ **BUCKLAND**
The Manor House
c1965 B368017

Buckland Manor was owned at one time by the Dukes of Suffolk, earning it its alternate title of the Duke's Manor. In 1544 it was sold to John Yate, who was then Merchant of the Staple at Calais. The Staple, in this instance, refers to a principle product of commerce, such as wool, and not to a small piece of wire.

► **BUCKLAND**
The Square and the Post Office
c1965 B368024

The post office and stores, seen here on the left, closed in the early 1980s when it was converted into a dwelling house. An earlier post office had been located in the row of houses seen on the left. The village lost its post office in 1997. The ivy on the house on the right is in the shape of a large cross.

BUCKLAND
The Village c1965
B368026

Buckland has some very
interesting thatched and
Georgian houses. The
village also has a Roman
Catholic and an Anglican
parish church, the
church of St Mary the
Virgin, which contains
manorial box pews,
brasses, hatchment
boards and an alabaster
carving of the Adoration
of the Shepherds.

CHILDREY, *The Village c1955* C287003

The Hatchet public house, seen on the left in the photograph, is still open for business today. A nearby road sign indicates
that there is a school nearby. A sign on the building directly behind the telegraph post indicates that a car service is
provided. It does not look like a garage, so one may assume that it was probably a taxi service.

GROVE
Grove Stores c1966
G131013

Grove, with its numerous housing estates, is one of the largest villages in the Vale of the White Horse. Its history, however, dates back to the time of King Stephen, when a manor was established here in the 12th century. Many inhabitants would have frequented the Grove Stores to buy a Wall's ice cream or perhaps post a letter.

EAST CHALLOW, *Main Road c1955* E89002

Here we see the main A417 Wantage to Faringdon road that runs through the village. On the grass verge on the right is an old water pump. Two motorcycles are parked outside the village pub, one leaning against the wall. Members of the Lovegrove family ran the Goodlake pub for over 130 years.

95

STEVENTON
The Green c1955
S606005

Steventon's village green is reputed to be one of the largest and finest in the county. Here we see children enjoying themselves on the swings and seesaw that existed at the time. Just beyond the seesaw you may see one of the goals of the football pitch. In summer, cricket is played on the green.

▼ **STEVENTON,** *The Causeway c1955* S606009

Although the photograph shows houses situated along part of the Causeway, the feature itself is just out of the picture on the left. The Causeway is a raised thoroughfare that was built centuries ago by monks from a local priory as part of the route that ran between the priory and Abingdon Abbey.

▶ **DRAYTON**
High Street c1960
D109008

The village of Drayton is situated two miles south of Abingdon. It was an agricultural centre for the area, and was once well known for its walnuts. The photograph shows an interesting row of cottages in the High Street. The porch of the cottages on the right is quite striking in that its tiles match those on the roof.

◄ DRAYTON
The Village c1960
D109011

We are at the junction of the High Street and Abingdon Road. A sign beside the finger-post road sign points the way to the premises of Ruddock & Meighan in the High Street. On the opposite side of the road a group of people are seen waiting for a bus. To their right is the 'cash stores' of E N Winfield; today the building houses Drayton post office.

► DRAYTON
Church Lane c1960 D109019

The tower of St Peter's Church was built in the 15th century. The Rev F E Robinson, a dedicated campanologist, was reputed to have rung the bells in every belfry in England. Inside the church there are some carvings that are attributed to him.

DRAYTON
The Wheatsheaf
c1965 D109027

It is reputed that Kimmeridge clay bricks, used to rebuild the village after it had been badly damaged by fire in the 19th century, were made behind the Wheatsheaf. Opposite the inn, on the village green, there is a stone cross that was erected for Queen Victoria's Golden Jubilee.

CULHAM, *The Church 1890* 27004

St Paul's Church, Culham is mainly Victorian, although the tower was rebuilt in 1710. The rowing boat, with its cushioned seat in the foreground appears to have been abandoned - although I suspect that its occupants are having a picnic on the bank of the Culham Cut.

CULHAM
The College 1900
45207

Bishop Samuel Wilberforce founded Culham College, a neo-Gothic training school for schoolmasters, in 1853. Its initial intake was to accommodate 130 students, and its first principal was a Welshman, Canon Ashwell. Situated in Thame Lane, the college closed in 1976. Two years later, in 1978, the Schola Europaea (European School) opened.

CULHAM, *The College Chapel 1900* 45210

Built in the grounds of the old Culham teacher training college, the chapel displays the connection between the college and the religious principle under which it was run and organised. The occupant of the deckchair on the left appears to have disappeared, no doubt because he/she found it difficult to hold a distant conversation with the man on the right.

► **CULHAM**
The Green c1955
C205005

Culham Stores, in the Burycroft, which is housed in the building just to the right of centre, has closed since this photograph was taken. It is now a private dwelling house. A sign on the village green advertises the Lion Inn. Once serving Morrell's ales, this has also closed.

◄ **CULHAM**
The Lock c1965 C205008

Pleasure boat trips on the Thames have been popular for many a year. Here we see the 'Wargrave' passing through the lock. It must have been a quiet time of the year, because there do not appear to be many passengers aboard. Culham Bridge can be seen beyond the lock.

▼ **SUTTON COURTENAY,** *The Bridge 1890* 27003

A tranquil River Thames flows beneath Sutton Bridge. The bridge replaced a ferry in 1811. Since 1809, when the Culham Cut was opened, the main river craft and leisure boats now bypass this part of the Thames.

► **SUTTON COURTENEY**
High Street c1955
S234005

Two ladies are pushing their prams along a very quiet High Street in Sutton Courteney. If you look very carefully behind the hedge on the left, you may just see the top of a telephone box. It seems a strange place to locate a kiosk.

◀ **SUTTON COURTENEY**
The Green c1955
S234007

In the churchyard of the village church of All Saints, whose Norman tower rises above the trees, can be found the grave of Eric Arthur Blair, better known as the novelist and essayist George Orwell, whose works include '1984' and 'Animal Farm'. Another celebrated person buried here is Herbert Henry Asquith, Liberal Prime Minister from 1908 to 1916.

▶ **HARWELL**
Jennings Lane c1960
H232001

Harwell has a long and chequered history, but it is probably better known for its Atomic Energy Research Establishment that was established nearby in 1946. Jennings Lane is named after a successful yeoman who lived in the village. He and his wife had twelve children. A brass memorial in the village church commemorates him - not necessarily for his progenitive achievement.

▶ **HARWELL**
Old Cottages c1960
H232010

In 1852 a great fire destroyed many of the old buildings and cottages in Harwell. A discharged labourer was reputed to have started the fire when he set a hayrick alight. Adnams Farm, where the event occurred, survived, and so did the attractive cottages captured by this delightful photograph.

◀ **HARWELL**
The Village Church c1960 H232029

The origins of the Church of St Matthew date back to the 13th century. Not far from the church is Prince's Manor. The manor was given to a Richard D'Oily by William the Conqueror, and was later given its current title by the Black Prince. The village has other manors, all with historical interest.

▲ **NORTH MORETON,** *The Queen Victoria c1950* N252001

The landlord of the Queen Victoria pub when this photograph was taken was Bert Pointer. In addition to supping a Morrell's ale you could also have a game of bar billiards. A notice on the fence advertises the film 'Blockheads', starring Laurel and Hardy, which would be showing at the new Coronet Cinema in Didcot.

◄ **NORTH MORETON**
The Village c1950
N252008

North Moreton still has many 15th-, 16th- and 17th-century buildings, including the one seen in the photograph. It was up for sale at that time. Amongst the village inhabitants during the 20th century was a certain R G Collingwood, who was described as being a most learned man.

▶ **SOUTH MORETON**
The Village c1940
S783002

The post holding the pub sign for the Crown, in Crown Lane, bears another sign that states 'pull in'. The inn, almost out of picture on the right, appears to have sold teas in addition to the more standard Ushers ales. Hilaire Belloc, the author, once lived in the village.

▶ *(far right) detail from*
S783002

◄ SOUTH MORETON
The Village c1940
S783006

The photograph shows the scene looking down Crown Lane. The Crown inn, mentioned in photograph S783002, is on the left at the far end. In addition to its delightful thatched houses, the village had a number of small businesses, which included a saddler and a blacksmith.

◄ *(far left) detail from*
S783006

▼ **SOUTH MORETON,** *The New Council Houses c1940* s783008

In contrast with the old, as seen in the other South Moreton photographs, we have here a row of new rather boxy-looking council houses. Plain and dull, they certainly do not have the attraction of the old thatched properties. Mind you, the garden sheds at the rear look somewhat antiquated.

► **EAST HAGBOURNE** *Main Road c1955* E90001

The Fleur-de-Lys public house, seen on the right in the photograph, is still open for business today. As its name suggests, Main Road is the main road through the village, which is situated almost on the outskirts of Didcot. It has some wonderful old houses, which unfortunately are not to be seen in this photograph.

EAST HAGBOURNE
St Andrew's Church c1955
E90004

Perched on the tower parapet of the church of St Andrew is a bell-cote, only just visible in this photograph, which houses its Sanctus bell. East Hagbourne is a fascinating village with a great number of 16th- and 17th-century houses with contrasting architectural styles. It also has two ancient stone crosses.

EAST HAGBOURNE
The Boot Inn c1955 E90005

The Boot Inn, seen on the right, has suffered the same fate as many other village inns, not only in Oxfordshire but in many other counties also, in that it has closed and been converted into a private house. With Didcot being so near, one will not go short of somewhere to drink a beer or two.

111

BLEWBURY
Green Bushes c1955
B737001

Blewbury is a village full of pleasant surprises; it has a surfeit of interesting cottages, many of which are thatched. Here we see a 16th-century un-thatched cottage with its rickety front gate. It once had a blacksmith's attached to it. The cottage was enlarged in 1976.

BLEWBURY, *Chapmans c1955* B737019

Many modern-day artists live in the village today, drawn here by the various architectural styles of the village's old buildings. The oldest houses have 15th- and 16th-century timber frames, some with box frames with large or small panels. Others have gable-end jetties. The fascination and variety never ends.

BLEWBURY
Turkeys c1955
B737020

Turkeys is another of the delightful 17th-century thatched cottages that can be found in the village. Many of the older houses were built using cob, a composition of clay, gravel and straw, and cob walls can still be seen here. Fire is always a threat, and Blewbury lost one of its attractive 16th-century cottages, Nottyngham Fee, fairly recently.

BLEWBURY, *Kealmwick Cottage c1955* B737010

We end our tour of Oxfordshire villages with this delightful 16th-century thatched cottage beside the Mill Brook. It is not difficult to see what attracted Dick Francis, ex-jockey and thriller writer, Kenneth Graham, author of 'The Wind in The Willows', and many others to have made their home in Blewbury during their lifetime.

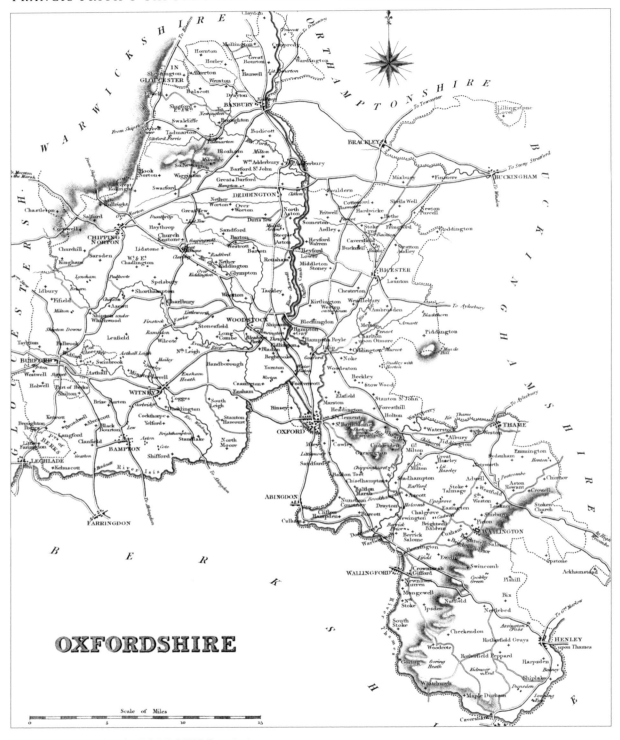

COUNTY MAP OF OXFORDSHIRE *c1850*

INDEX

Adderbury 64, 65

Ascott-under-Wychwood 80

Bampton 86-87

Barford St Michael 60-61

Benson 25, 26-27, 28-29

Bladon 78-79

Blewbury 112, 113

Bloxham 61, 62-63, 64-65

Broughton 65, 66-67, 68-69

Buckland 92-93, 94

Childrey 94

Chislehampton 39, 40-41

Cholsey 23

Clifton Hampden 34-35, 36-37

Cropredy 70-71, 72

Cuddesdon 46, 47

Culham 100, 101, 102-103

Deddington 58-59

Dorchester 31, 34

Drayton 98-99, 100

Ducklington 82-83, 84-85

East Challow 95

East Hagbourne 110-111

Ewlelme 23, 24, 25

Garsington 44-45, 46-47

Great Haseley 50

Great Tew 75, 76

Grove 95

Harwell 105, 106-107

Horley 72, 73

Little Haseley 51

Little Milton 48-49

Lower Heyford 52-53, 54-55

Mapledurham 15, 18-19

Minster Lovell 82-83

Moulsford 20-21

Nettlebed 20, 21

North Moreton 107

North Stoke 22

Nuneham Courtenay 38-39

Radcot 87

Salford 74

Sandford-on-Thames 42-43, 44

Shillingford 30

Shiplake 14, 15

Shipton-under-Wychwood 81

Shorhampton 80

Shrivenham 88

Souldern 57, 58

South Moreton 108-109, 110

South Stoke 22

Stadhampton 40, 41, 42-43

Steeple Aston 55, 56, 57

Steventon 12, 96-97, 98

Sutton Courtenay 104-105

Tackley 76-77

Uffington 90, 91, 92

Warborough 28, 29, 30

Watchfield 89

Woolstone 89, 90

ACKNOWLEDGEMENTS

I should like to acknowledge the help and assistance received at the Centre For Oxfordshire Studies at Oxford Central Library; from the staff at various Tourist Information Centres; and from the many residents who provided me with information during my tour of Oxfordshire.

FRITH PRODUCTS & SERVICES

Francis Frith would doubtless be pleased to know that the pioneering publishing venture he started in 1860 still continues today. Over a hundred and forty years later, The Francis Frith Collection continues in the same innovative tradition and is now one of the foremost publishers of vintage photographs in the world. Some of the current activities include:

INTERIOR DECORATION

Today Frith's photographs can be seen framed and as giant wall murals in thousands of pubs, restaurants, hotels, banks, retail stores and other public buildings throughout the country. In every case they enhance the unique local atmosphere of the places they depict and provide reminders of gentler days in an increasingly busy and frenetic world.

PRODUCT PROMOTIONS

Frith products are used by many major companies to promote the sales of their own products or to reinforce their own history and heritage. Frith promotions have been used by Hovis bread, Courage beers, Scots Porage Oats, Colman's mustard, Cadbury's foods, Mellow Birds coffee, Dunhill pipe tobacco, Guinness, and Bulmer's Cider.

GENEALOGY AND FAMILY HISTORY

As the interest in family history and roots grows world-wide, more and more people are turning to Frith's photographs of Great Britain for images of the towns, villages and streets where their ancestors lived; and, of course, photographs of the churches and chapels where their ancestors were christened, married and buried are an essential part of every genealogy tree and family album.

FRITH PRODUCTS

All Frith photographs are available Framed or just as Mounted Prints and Posters (size 23 x 16 inches). These may be ordered from the address below. Other products available are - Address Books, Calendars, Jigsaws, Canvas Prints, Postcards and local and prestige books.

THE INTERNET

Already ninety thousand Frith photographs can be viewed and purchased on the internet through the Frith websites and a myriad of partner sites.

For more detailed information on Frith products, look at this site:
www.francisfrith.com

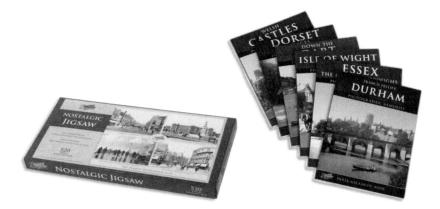

See the complete list of Frith Books at: www.francisfrith.com
This web site is regularly updated with the latest list of publications from The Francis Frith Collection. If you wish to buy books relating to another part of the country that your local bookshop does not stock, you may purchase on-line.

For further information, trade, or author enquiries please contact us at the address below:
The Francis Frith Collection, Unit 6, Oakley Business Park, Wylye Road, Dinton, Wiltshire SP3 5EU.
Tel: +44 (0)1722 716 376 Fax: +44 (0)1722 716 881 Email: sales@francisfrith.co.uk

---

See Frith products on the internet at www.francisfrith.com

FREE PRINT OF YOUR CHOICE

Mounted Print
Overall size 14 x 11 inches (355 x 280mm)

Choose any Frith photograph in this book.
Simply complete the Voucher opposite and return it with your remittance for £3.50 (to cover postage and handling) and we will print the photograph of your choice in SEPIA (size 11 x 8 inches) and supply it in a cream mount with a burgundy rule line (overall size 14 x 11 inches).
Please note: aerial photographs and photographs with a reference number starting with a "Z" are not Frith photographs and cannot be supplied under this offer. Offer valid for delivery to one UK address only.

PLUS: Order additional Mounted Prints at HALF PRICE - £9.50 each (normally £19.00)
If you would like to order more Frith prints from this book, possibly as gifts for friends and family, you can buy them at half price (with no additional postage and handling costs).

PLUS: Have your Mounted Prints framed
For an extra £18.00 per print you can have your mounted print(s) framed in an elegant polished wood and gilt moulding, overall size 16 x 13 inches (no additional postage and handling required).

IMPORTANT!

These special prices are only available if you use this form to order. You must use the ORIGINAL VOUCHER on this page (no copies permitted). We can only despatch to one UK address. This offer cannot be combined with any other offer.

Send completed Voucher form to:
The Francis Frith Collection, Unit 6, Oakley Business Park, Wylye Road, Dinton, Wiltshire SP3 5EU

CHOOSE A PHOTOGRAPH FROM THIS BOOK

Voucher for **FREE** and Reduced Price *Frith Prints*

Please do not photocopy this voucher. Only the original is valid, so please fill it in, cut it out and return it to us with your order.

Picture ref no	Page no	Qty	Mounted @ £9.50	Framed + £18.00	Total Cost £
		1	Free of charge*	£	£
			£9.50	£	£
			£9.50	£	£
			£9.50	£	£
			£9.50	£	£
			£9.50	£	£
Please allow 28 days for delivery. Offer available to one UK address only			* Post & handling		£3.80
			Total Order Cost		£

Title of this book . . . .

I enclose a cheque/postal order for £ . . . .
made payable to 'The Francis Frith Collection'

OR please debit my Mastercard / Visa / Maestro card, details below

Card Number:

Issue No (Maestro only):   Valid from (Maestro):

Card Security Number: Expires:

Signature:

Name Mr/Mrs/Ms . . . .

Address . . . .

. . . .

. . . .

. . . . Postcode . . . .

Daytime Tel No . . . .

Email . . . .

Valid to 31/12/12

Can you help us with information about any of the Frith photographs in this book?

We are gradually compiling an historical record for each of the photographs in the Frith archive. It is always fascinating to find out the names of the people shown in the pictures, as well as insights into the shops, buildings and other features depicted.

If you recognize anyone in the photographs in this book, or if you have information not already included in the author's caption, do let us know. We would love to hear from you, and will try to publish it in future books or articles.

An Invitation from The Francis Frith Collection to Share Your Memories

The 'Share Your Memories' feature of our website allows members of the public to add personal memories relating to the places featured in our photographs, or comment on others already added. Seeing a place from your past can rekindle forgotten or long held memories. Why not visit the website, find photographs of places you know well and add YOUR story for others to read and enjoy? We would love to hear from you!

www.francisfrith.com/memories

Our production team

Frith books are produced by a small dedicated team at offices near Salisbury. Most have worked with the Frith Collection for many years. All have in common one quality: they have a passion for the Frith Collection.

Frith Books and Gifts

We have a wide range of books and gifts available on our website utilising our photographic archive, many of which can be individually personalised.

www.francisfrith.com